AF257117

The Resurrection

Minister Glendora ShanThomas

Copyright © 2023 Janna Hurd

ISBN 978-1-7330579-7-4
Sivad Publishing
www.tamathaadavis.com

Printed in USA by Ingram Spark
First printing August 2023

Cover Art by **Scotti Taylor**
Edited by **Heidi Bjork**

All scripture references are bolded. All 12 COVENANTS ARE BOLDED AND IN ALL CAPS. *"All scripture quotations are bolded, italicized and in quotes".*

Unless otherwise indicated All scriptures are taken from the King James Version Bible 1604 & 1611 *(Public Domain)*

All rights reserved. No part of this book may be reproduced or transmitted in any form or by any means without written permission from the author.

The Resurrection

Minister Glendora ShanThomas

Dedication

This book is dedicated to our mom, Glendora Shan Thomas, and published in her memory for the advancement of the kingdom of Our Lord.

-Thomas Family

Table of Contents

Chapter One

J esus rode into the city of

Jerusalem at the time of the feast of the Passover on a donkey. He did this to fulfill the prophecy in Zachariah, **Matthew 21:4-5** *"All this was done, that it might be fulfilled which was spoken by the prophet, saying, Tell ye the daughter of Sion, Behold, thy King cometh unto thee, meek, and sitting upon an ass, and a colt the foal of an ass."***(Zachariah 9:9)**

Jesus came to Jerusalem at this time knowing that it was the divine time

appointed for his death, burial, and Resurrection. He knew that both governments would take counsel against Him and together they would crucify Him before the feast of the Passover because they believed that His death would destroy His ministry.

Jesus had to identify Himself as the **MESSIAH** of the people. To the people, because they were devoted believers, who understood the signs and events that were happening at the time, and they lived in expectation of the coming of the **MESSIAH**. They knew that the signs fulfilled the prophecies of His coming.

The Samaritans, who lived in the village where Jesus met the woman at the well, believed that the current events were enough evidence that the **MESSIAH** had come. In the conversation with Jesus, she told Him, *"I know that the Messiah cometh, which is called the Christ, when He is come, He will tell all things. Jesus saith unto her, I that speak unto thee am He."* (John 4:25-26)

As soon as the multitudes in Jerusalem acknowledged that it was Jesus who rode on the donkey, they began to worship Him, and laid palms

in the streets before Him as He entered into the city. They also spread their garments along the road, singing ***"Hosanna to the son of David: Blessed is he that comes in the name of the Lord; Hosanna in the highest."*** **(Matthew 21:6-11)**

During that week of preparation for the feast of the Passover, Jesus went into the temple and drove out all the money changers and all the merchants who sold animals for sacrifice. **(Matthew 21:12)**

Jesus stayed in the temple, and the courtyards of the temple to minister

to the people who were gathered there to listen to Him.

But on the festive occasions, the chief priests, the Pharisees. their disciples with the Herodians, and the Sadducees were kept busy. They tempted Jesus with arguments about religion, and the law. But on this particular occasion the Pharisees sought to involve Him in politics against the Roman government. They asked Jesus: ***"Is it lawful to give tribute unto Caesar, or not?"*** (Matthew 22:15-22)

But Jesus never committed Himself to

their game, the Pharisees had failed to incriminate Jesus with the Romans. The Sadducees became angrier and decided to attack Jesus openly on the doctrine of the Resurrection. The Sadducees never believed in the Resurrection.

They came to Jesus with a story about a woman who is married to seven brothers according to the law of Inheritance in the covenant of **Peace. *(The law of Moses)* (Deuteronomy 25:5 -12)**

Each brother was married to the woman hoping to produce an heir to

the family's name because her first husband, their first brother died before he had an heir to the family's name. **(Matthew 22:23 - 32)**

The Sadducees used this example to disregard the principle of the doctrine of the Resurrection.

Neither did they regard the old law of the Melchizedek priesthood of their forefathers Abraham, Isaac, and Jacob. Because it was on the same principle of marriage for inheritance, that Judah's daughter in law, Tamar, the widow of his first son, tricked him into sleeping with her. And from this union,

Tamar, gave birth to Pharez and Zarah twin brothers. **(Genesis 38:1-30)**

Pharez: The firstborn son of the twin brothers, became the patriarch, and high priest of the tribe of Judah after the death of his Father Judah. **(Luke 3:33)**

The descendants of Pharez are recorded among the high priests of the Melchizedek priesthood in the genealogy of Jesus the Christ. **(Luke 3:23 - 38)**

For even in the Melchizedek priesthood, they believe in the doctrine of the Resurrection.

Job, Melchizedek high priest, confirmed that they believe in the Resurrection saying, *"For I know that my redeemer liveth, and that he shall stand at the latter day upon the earth: And though after my skin worms destroy this body, yet in my flesh shall I see Whom I shall see for myself, and mine eyes shall behold, and not another, though my reins be consumed within me.* (Job 19:25 - 27)

Jesus answered the Sadducees saying: ***"Ye do err, not knowing the scriptures, nor the power of God. For in the resurrection, they neither marry, nor are given in marriage, but are as the angels of God in heaven."*** **(Matthew 22:29, 30)**

Jesus' statement to the Sadducees is a revelation from God, to us, His children. Jesus taught us through this statement how we shall be in the Resurrection. We know from our LORD Jesus' statement to the Sadducees that we shall be like the angels in the Resurrection. That is to say without any GENDER (male or female).

Because in the Resurrection there will be no need for union in marriage. God instituted marriage to create families. But in the Resurrection, there is no need to multiply and replenish the earth as God commanded all mankind in creation. **(Genesis 1:28)**

Therefore, when we speak of women in ministry for Jesus' church, we speak of called servants of God, who shall serve God's temple forever with our High Priest Jesus. In the resurrection, everyone will be like angels, without GENDER.

Therefore every called woman and man of God who ministers in God's temple with our high priest Jesus will serve God like angels. The apostle Paul instructed the Ephesian ministers about being called a vessel of God by predestination. ***"Paul, an apostle of Jesus Christ by the will of God, to the saints which are at Ephesus, and to the faithful in Christ Jesus: Grace be to you, and peace, from God our Father, and from the Lord Jesus Christ. Blessed be the God and Father of our Lord Jesus Christ, who hath blessed us with all spiritual blessings in heavenly places in Christ: According as he hath chosen us in him before the***

foundation of the world, that we should be holy and without blame before him in love: [5] Having predestined us unto the adoption of children by Jesus Christ to himself, according to the good pleasure of His will, To the praise of the glory of His grace, wherein He hath made us accepted in the beloved. In whom we have redemption through His blood, the forgiveness of sins, according to the riches of his grace; (Ephesians 1: 1- 7)

The apostle Paul had instructed the Ephesian ministers about being called a vessel of God by predestination

(Ephesians 1:1-7) And he also instructed the Roman ministers concerning the same issue of being called by God to serve him by predestination saying:*"For whom He did foreknow, He also did predestinate to be conformed to the image of his Son, that He might be the firstborn among many brethren. Moreover, whom He did predestinate, whom He also called: and whom He called, whom He also justified: and whom He justified, whom He also glorified."* **(Romans 8:29, 30)** Jesus created a new priesthood for His church on the earth. A priesthood of called women and men. *"For whosoever shall call*

upon the name of the Lord shall be saved." (Romans 10:13)

This **WORD** of **SALVATION** is according to the **WORD** of the covenant of **Remission**:
"For God so loved the world that He gave his only begotten son, that whoever believes in Him, shall not perish, but have everlasting life." (John 3:16)

Chapter Two

 B ut the **WORDS** Jesus revealed to the Sadducees concerning **ANGELS** is impressive!

Yet still, a dark cloud hovers over the Church. It is imminent in the hearts of many ministers, who teach that the holy Scriptures contradicts itself.

These ministers contradict Jesus' **WORD**, saying that the translation about evil angels in the book of Genesis is wrong. They contend that the **WORD** of **God** cannot speak of evil

angels, who came into the earth to marry daughters of men, just to reproduce a superhuman race of angels without gender.

They contend against the scripture saying: *(How did evil angels have children with daughters of men in the days of Noah?)* :" **And it came to pass, when men began to multiply on the face of the earth, and daughters were born unto them, That the sons of God saw the daughters of men that they were fair; and they took them wives of all which they chose. And the Lord said My spirit shall not always strive with man, for that he**

also is flesh: yet his days shall be
an hundred and twenty years.
4 There were giants in the earth in
those days; and also, after that,
when the sons of God came in unto
the daughters of men, and they
bore children to them, the same
became mighty men which were of
old, men of renown. And God saw
that the wickedness of man was
great in the earth, and that every
imagination of the thoughts of his
heart was only evil continually.
6 And it repented the Lord that He
had made man on the earth, and it
grieved Him at His heart. And
the Lord said, I will destroy man
whom I have created from the face

of the earth; both man, and beast, and the creeping thing, and the fowls of the air; for it repenteth me that I have made them. (Genesis 6:1-7)

But as children of God, we believe that God 's **WORD** is **true**, according to the scripture: David sang in praise to the Lord saying: *"Thy WORD is true from the very beginning."* **(Psalms 119:160)** Jesus prayed and proclaimed the covenant of **LIFE** saying to the Father *"Sanctify them through the truth; thy WORD is truth*. **(John 17:17)**

Jesus spoke about the power of the **WORD** of **God** and every one of His instructions throughout His ministry. After the apostle Peter made the revelation of Jesus, being the Christ of God, the Father at the retreat into Caesarea Philippi, Jesus taught them this truth: ***"For whosoever shall be ashamed of me and my WORDS, of Him shall the Son of man shall be ashamed, when he shall come in His own glory, and His Fathers and in the holy angels."*** **(Luke 9:26)**

As a consequence of seeking wisdom of God, a child of God will have no

need to doubt and continue the
WORD of **God,** Our Father.

Because we believe because we have
no need to doubt and contain the
WORD of **God**, because we believe
above all things that God 's **WORD** is
true! The holy **WORD** of **God** is His
written covenant to mankind, the
scripture. All of God's covenants are
established forever!

Knowing this truth, we seek wisdom.
We seek the wisdom of God for the
spiritual understanding in the
mysteries of God - the Holy Spirit, who
is appointed to us by God to enlighten

us, teach us, and guide us into our **righteousness** of His.

We therefore understand that angels are spirits who live in the spirit world with God. They are sent from God to minister onto earth to and for His children. This is the **WORD** of the apostle Paul to the Hebrew church *"**Are they not all ministering spirits sent forth to minister for them who shall be heirs of salvation?**"***(Hebrews 1:14)** David said that an angel protects everyone who fears the Lord or loves the Lord. *"**The angel of the Lord encamps around**"*

them that fear him and delivers them. (Psalm 34:7)

- Angels are also ministers with Jesus in the temple in heaven.

- We know this from the prophecy in the book of Revelation.

- So then, in order for us to understand the mystery of the evil angels with the daughters of men, we must first understand that his spirit cannot operate on his own in the natural world.

- A spirit must have a body which it will operate in the natural world.
- Therefore, a spirit can find a body whose spirit is open and available to receive it.
- Then the evil spirit, or demon becomes interested in possessing the spirit, and soul of that individual.
- It dictates the thoughts and actions of the individual.
- The individual then becomes the personification of the demon, the body.

- Demons are evil spirits from hell. They are evil angels or devils from hell.
- These evil angels were thrown out of heaven with Satan. **(Luke 10:18) (Revelation 12:7 - 9)**
- **(Matthew 8:32) (Matthew 12:45)**

Therefore, the question is, who are these evil angels that possess men's bodies in order to produce superhuman beings with daughters of men?

And the answer is in the scripture which tells us in no uncertain terms: that these evil angels were thrown out of heaven with Satan **(Revelation 12:7 - 9)**

- They came to the earth with him to destroy mankind.
- Remember always, that's in disguise inside the body of a serpent. **(Genesis 3:1)**
- These evil angels went out on the mission to stop God's divine plan of salvation to all mankind.
- The super beings, born from other human beings, were born in corruption.

- This corruption was intended to illuminate the natural birth and function of all mankind. **(Genesis 6:1-7)**
- This corruption would not give birth to the seed of the woman. **(Genesis 3:15)**
- The seed of the woman was born to bruise the head of the serpent. **(Genesis 3:15)**
- The Son of God is the seed of the woman.
- He came into the earth to destroy the works of the devil.
- For this purpose, the Son of God was manifested, that He

may destroy the works of the devil. **(1 John 3:8)**

- The Lord God came down to earth and destroyed this evil in the times of Noah.

- He spoke the flood into existence, and

- He destroyed the world of these evil beings that ruled the earth at that time.

- He destroyed the generation of super beings, and women from the earth.

- Satan's plan to destroy mankind from being a natural born human being according to

the will of God, the Father, was completely destroyed forever.

- Only Noah, the servant of God, with his family, and every living thing that was placed into the arc were saved. **(Genesis 6- 9).**

Chapter Three

This flood brought a new beginning which established a new covenant between God, and mankind. Every new beginning establishes a new covenant between God and mankind.

This new covenant was the covenant of **JUDGMENT**, which is established between the LORD, the Lord God, Our advocate of our covenants with the Father; and Noah, the Melchizedek high priest.

The LORD God said to Noah, *"I will*

establish my covenant with you; neither shall all flesh be cut off anymore by waters of a flood; neither shall there be any more a flood to destroy the earth."
(Genesis 9:11)

Let's look at a new beginning that brought the mercies of God to mankind - God 's covenants:

1: "In the beginning was the **WORD**, and the **WORD** was **with God** and the WORD **was God. (John 1:1)**

- This **WORD** was the **first WORD**,

- or the first spoken **WORD** by God,
- to create the world, and all mankind.
- **Spoken WORD by God** is the **Rhema WORD** of **God.**

This **WORD** was the **first covenant of God** for the creation of mankind.
This **WORD** is **SALVATION.**
So, the **first covenant** between **God** and M**ANKIND** is the covenant of **SALVATION**

The name of Jesus means **SAVIOR,** or **SALVATION**.

"The same was in the beginning with God, All things were made by him, and without him there was not anything made that was made. (John 1:3)

This **WORD, SALVATION** is the Son of God. John said: ***"And the Word was made flesh, and dwelt among us, (and we beheld his glory, the glory as of the only begotten of the Father,) full of grace and truth.*** (John 1:14)

Jesus is the covenant **WORD** salvation. He wasn't manifested in the world by **God** for the redemption of all mankind. He is the Lamb of God slain

from the foundation of the world for the redemption of all mankind. **(Revelation 13:8)**

God, the Father calls things into being. **(Genesis 1:1 - 31)** The Lord God, or God, the Son made all things. He fashioned him. God, the Father rested from all his work on the seventh day. **(Genesis 2:3)**

After God rested on the seventh day, we find that the following verse speaks of the generations of heaven and earth saying: ***"These are the generations of heaven and earth, when they were created; in the day,***

the Lord God made the heavens and the earth. (Genesis 2:4)

The Lord God, the Son of God made all things that the Father called into being. The apostle Saint John said, *"All things were made by him and without him there was nothing there was not anything that was made."* (John 1:3)

Paul says *"But we speak the wisdom of God in a mystery, even the hidden wisdom which God ordained before the world onto our glory."*(1 Corinthians 2:7)

Jesus is the mystery of God,

manifested in the air as a divine appointment to fulfill the first covenant in His own **WORDS** for the salvation of all mankind. John the Baptist reveals Jesus' true identity by revelation from God when he welcomes Jesus into his congregation saying: ***"Behold the Lamb of God."*** **(John 1:29)**

Chapter Four

$\mathcal{A}$s the divine appointment time for the manifestation of the Son of God approached, God provided a body for Him. He was born of the virgin, Mary. With a manifestation of the Son of God, the apostle Paul reminded them about the prophetic WORD of king David saying: ***"Wherefore when he cometh into the world, he saith, Sacrifice and offering thou wouldest not, but a body hast thou prepared me:*** **(Hebrews 10:5) (Psalm 40:6-7)**

1 - Jesus fulfilled the first covenant with his blood on the cross. He was sacrificed as a lamb to the slaughter, so that we might have **LIFE** in the kingdom of God forever. **(Isaiah 53:7)** Jesus is our advocate to the Father. He is our high priest and intercessor with the Father. This is why we pray in the name of Jesus.

2 - The second covenant was established in the Garden of Eden between Adam, and the Lord, the Lord God. **(Genesis 3:1 - 24)** This is the covenant of **REDEMPTION**. This brought the first manifestation of blood into the earth. The Lord, the

Lord God sacrificed animals in the Garden of Eden and Adam and Eve lost their covering of the glory of God because of sin, and the transgressions against the **WORD** of the Lord God.

What is the manifestation of the mystery of God, which gives **LIFE** to the body of every living thing on the earth? Adam was the first, Melchizedek, the priest of the earth.

3 - The third covenant between the Lord, the Lord God was the covenant of **JUDGMENT**, between the Lord, the Lord God and Noah. **(Genesis 5:30 - 32)**

4 - For the fourth covenant was between the Lord, the Lord God and Abram. The Lord God told Abram to leave his father's house, and his homeland to go to a new land. This was the new beginning which would give birth to the new nation, who will serve him, and not idols. This is the covenant of **BLESSING. (Genesis 12:1 - 7)**

5 - The fifth covenant confirms the new nation, and the promised land, which will be for the descendants of Abram. **(Genesis 15:9 - 18)** In spite of not having the seeds that were

promised to him that will give him the nation, Abram believed the Lord God, and obeyed him. The Lord God counted Abram's love and faith for him as righteousness. Abram established the fifth covenant of **RIGHTEOUSNESS** with the Lord God. **(Genesis 15:18)** The covenant of **RIGHTEOUSNESS** is the only covenant which speaks of a civic dispensation of time; 400 years. **(Genesis 15:13)**

6 - Abram established the sixth covenant of **SANCTIFICATION**, which is the mark of the circumcision of every male child of the new nation, the seed of Abram. **(Genesis 17:1 - 27)** This

covenant changed Abram's name to Abraham - the father of many nations. This covenant was made with Abraham's blood. He cut himself to establish the covenant with the Lord God. **(Genesis 17:24)**

7 - Isaac was a young man when the Lord God sent Abraham to sacrifice him. **(Genesis 22:1 - 23)** Abraham obeyed the Lord God and took Isaac to the place where the Lord told him to make the sacrifice. This was Abraham's ultimate proof of his faith in the word of the LORD God for his life. The Lord that established the seventh covenant, with Abraham the

covenant of **FAITH**. He saw the Resurrection as his seed of Thomas, who would be the blessing of our nation. **(Hebrews 11:17 - 19)**

8 - The children of Jacob, the seed of Abraham, lived in the land of Egypt for 430 years. After these 430 years, the Lord God sent Moses, His prophet, and delivered them from the bondage of the Egyptians. **(Exodus 12:40)** This was the beginning of the new nation. Moses established the eighth covenant, **DELIVERANCE**, with the Lord God which brought the seed of Abraham out of Egypt for a new

beginning in the promised land.
(Exodus 12:1 - 52)

9 - The new priesthood for the new
nation was established between
Moses and the Lord, the Lord God at
Marah. **(Exodus 15:25 - 27)** under the
covenant, **HEALING**.

10 - The new nation was established
as a sovereign nation in the world
when Moses established the 10th
covenant with the Lord God. The Lord,
the Lord God established the 10th
covenant, **PEACE** in the wilderness of
Sinai with a nation of Israel. The law of
the 10 Commandments established

the nation of Israel a sovereign nation in all the world. **(Exodus 20-24)**

11- Jesus came to make the new beginning with God for the salvation of all mankind. He came to establish the covenant of a **REMISSION OF SINS**. He came to redeem unto God in his own blood. The covenant of a **REMISSION** was not made with animal blood. It was made with the blood of Jesus.

12 - Jesus shed His blood and established the covenant of **LIFE**, while He was on the cross. He carries the mark of this covenant on His side. A

Roman soldier pierced Jesus' side. Even though Jesus was already dead, blood and water came from the wound. The wound on Jesus' side marks the seal of the covenant of **LIFE**.

The covenant of **LIFE** marks the beginning of the new generation of the children of God. The children of God are born again in the Spirit of God. *"For as many as are led by the Spirit of God, they are the sons of God."* (Romans 8:14)

John told us: *"And as many received him, to them gave his power to become the sons of God even to*

them that believed in His name. Which we were born not of blood, nor by the will of flesh, nor of the will of man, but of God"(John 1:13)

The **12 Rhema WORDS of God** before the foundation of the world:

1. Salvation
2. Redemption
3. Judgment
4. Blessing
5. Righteousness
6. Sanctification
7. Faith
8. Deliverance
9. Healing

10. Peace
11. Remission
12. Life

These are the **WORDS** of the covenants of God with mankind. The covenant of God is the **SURE WORD of God** to mankind.

Chapter Five

We are in the last days because all covenants have been fulfilled. The mystery of God from the foundation of the world has been revealed, Jesus Christ, God, the Son of Our High Priest of heaven and earth. God, our Father has redeemed unto Him - the blood of His Son.

Isaiah, the prophet speaks about the Resurrection saying: ***"Say to them that are of a fearful heart, Be strong, fear not: behold, your God***

will come with vengeance, even God with a recompense; he will come and save you. [5] Then the eyes of the blind shall be opened, and the ears of the deaf shall be unstopped. [6] Then shall the lame man leap as a hart, and the tongue of the dumb sing: for in the wilderness shall waters break out, and streams in the desert. And the parched ground shall become a pool, and the thirsty land springs of water: in the habitation of dragons, where each lay, shall be grass with reeds and rushes. [8] And a highway shall be there, and a way, and it shall be called The way of holiness; the unclean shall not

pass over it; but it shall be for those: the wayfaring men, though fools, shall not err therein. ⁹ No lion shall be there, nor any ravenous beast shall go up thereon, it shall not be found there; but the redeemed shall walk there: ¹⁰ And the ransomed of the Lord *shall return and come to Zion with songs and everlasting joy upon their heads: they shall obtain joy and gladness, and sorrow and sighing shall flee away."* (Isaiah 35:4-10)

It would seem as if the topic of the Resurrection became an issue of controversy within the ministry of the

body of Christ from the very beginning. It is still used as a distraction to the importance of the Resurrection of Jesus Christ

Why is it so important that every minister should know, and understand the Resurrection? Because we should be able to preach and teach about the Resurrection of our Lord Jesus with spiritual understanding from the Holy Spirit.

Jesus said to the apostles at the retreat at Caesarea Philippi: ***"But I tell you of a truth, there be some standing here, which shall not***

taste of death, til they see the kingdom of God." (Luke 9:27)

"Then after eight days, Jesus took Peter, James, and John up into a mountain with him while he prayed. And as he prayed his countenance was altered, and his arraignment was white and glistening. And behold there talked with him two men, which were Moses and Elijah: which appeared in glory and spake of his decrease which he should accomplish at Jerusalem." (Luke 9:29:31)

Jesus stood before God, the Father as a priest, as a Christ, the anointed man

of God dressed in his holy priestly garments. Jesus dresses with the garments of a priest of His ministry. He never dressed as a high priest of heaven. Now He came to present himself to the Father as in the day of atonement, and the glory of God overwhelmed Him, and His garments became white and bright.

They found Jesus as He would return to them in His resurrection. Shining in the glory of God in the glorious perfect body of the resurrected Lord and King. The first begotten of the dead.

This was the transfiguration of Jesus' body. His body became the perfect body which God ordained from the creation of man. (Man and woman) and this would be the transfiguration of our bodies in the resurrection, the perfect body of Adam before sin and transgression overpower his **LIFE.**

The apostle Paul says the following concerning the Resurrection to focus our attention on the importance of knowing and understanding it so that we are able to teach it to the church. Every child of God should have an

understanding of how we all shall be at the coming of the Lord.

The Greek ministers, and believers cannot believe or accept the concept of the Resurrection of our Lord Jesus Christ. This is why they oppose the apostle with so many arguments in contentions.

The apostle Paul contended with the Corinthian ministers on this issue. In one of his arguments about the Resurrection of Jesus, and our Christian faith, Paul reminded me and the ministers that the Resurrection is the foundation of our faith in the

Gospel. This is the shield of our faith.

We firmly believe that Jesus will come again to receive the church into His care, and this will be in the Resurrection. Paul told him the following: *"And if Christ be not raised, your faith is vain; ye are yet in your sins."*(1 Corinthians 15:17)

Paul talks to them about the change from the present condition of our bodies, in regard to the resurrection saying:'' *Now this I say, brethren, that flesh and blood cannot inherit the kingdom of God; neither doth corruption inherit incorruption.*

Behold I show you a mystery. We shall not all sleep, but we shall all be changed in a moment, in the twinkling of an eye, at the last Trump for the trumpet shall sound, and the dead shall be raised incorruptible, and we shall be changed. For this corruptible must put on in corruption, in the mortal must put on a mortality. So when this corruptible shall put on incorruption, and this mortal shall put on a mortality, then shall be brought to pass the saying that is written, death is swallowed up in victory." (1 Corinthians 15:50-54)

The apostle Paul contends with the

Philippian ministers on the same issue saying to them, *"For our conversation is in heaven; from whence also we look for the Savior, the Lord Jesus Christ. Who shall change your veil body, but it may be fashioned like unto his glorious body, according to the working whereby he is able to subdue all things unto himself?"* (Philippians 3:20, 21)

Paul taught the ministers on the resurrection saying: *"But I would not have you to be ignorant, brethren, concerning them which are asleep, that ye sorrow not, even as others which have no hope. For if we*

believe that Jesus died and rose again, even so also which sleep in Jesus will God bring with him. For this we say unto you by the word of the Lord, that we which are alive and remain unto the coming of the Lord shall not prevent them which are asleep. For the Lord himself shall descend from heaven with a shout, with the voice of the archangel, and with the trump of God: and the dead in Christ shall rise first."
(1 Thessalonians 4:13-16)

Even ministers who were under the

ministry of Timothy and were controversial about the doctrine of resurrection taught the believers in their congregation that a Resurrection had already passed.

How shall Timothy avoid the conversations which were not becoming a minister of the gospel of our Lord Jesus Christ? ***"But shun profane and vain babblings: for they will increase unto more ungodliness And their word will eat as doth a canker: of whom is Hymenaeus and Philetus; Who concerning the truth have erred,***

saying that the resurrection is past already; and overthrow the faith of some. **(2 Timothy 2:16-18)** These are the contentions that are imminent in the church among ministers who are demonstrating strong influence in their beliefs in this controversy.

Some of the arguments concern Jesus' marriage with his family to prove without a shadow of a doubt that He did not die and could not have had a Resurrection.

Some of them still believe that His disciples took His body from the cross. These ministers are influenced by false

conceptions, and not by the holy Word of God.

This message that denies Jesus' Resurrection began with the authorities in Jerusalem after the soldiers told him that Jesus' body was not in the tomb. They said the disciples came by night and removed Jesus' body from the tomb. **(Matthew 28:11-15)**

The same authorities were afraid of the Resurrection of Jesus Christ because they knew that Jesus was a

prophet sent from God. Some of them thought that he was the Messiah, but they were not sure. This is why the apostle Paul told the Corinthians the following: ***"Which none of the princes of this world knew; for had they known it, they would not have crucified the Lord of glory."*** (1 Corinthians 2:8)

They opposed him with the people from the beginning of his ministry; and sought to kill him immediately after he whipped the money changers, and merchants who sell animals for sacrifices from the temple. Then Jesus told them: ***"Destroy this temple and***

in three days I will raise it up." **(John 2:19)** This was a principal accusation which the people used to bring him to trial for treason against their faith. The people accused Jesus saying: we heard him say destroy the temple that is made with hands, and within three days I will build another made with hands, but **"Jesus answered and said unto them:** *Destroy the temple and in three days I will raise it up,"* **(John 2:19)**

Chapter Six

Remember always that we are ambassadors for the living God, and our Lord Jesus Christ, therefore ministers of the gospel. We do not permit strange perceptions, and conceptions to overpower our

thoughts and minds and spiritual determination in our labor for the Lord Jesus Christ. We must preach salvation to a dying world!

Don't let derogatory arguments corrupt our minds. We are the servants of God, and the children of God. We are the children of God by the will of God.

The apostle John said:*" but as many as received him, to them gave him power to become the sons of God, even to them that believe on His name: which were born, not a blood, nor of the will of the flesh, nor the will of man, but of God."* **(John 1:12, 13)**

Our Lord and Savior, Jesus, gave us the example of faith and obedience to God's word and commandments. He was obedient to God even onto his death on the cross.

Jesus gave the ministry of the church a holy commission to fulfill until He returns for His church without spot or wrinkle.

When Jesus returns:
1.	The church of Jesus Christ will not be in controversy over His resurrection.
 2.	Nor will it be over His virgin birth. arguments

3.	The church of Jesus Christ will not be in disbelief regarding His ascension.

4.	This church without spot or wrinkle will be a believing church in the holy Word of God.

5.	It will be a church obedient to the will of God our Father, according to the instructions and admonition of the Holy Spirit, who was sent from God to be the comforter of the ministry of the church on the day of Pentecost, and forever more.

This is why every minister of Jesus Christ must know his or her

admonition in ministry. Our admonition in ministry is the holy commission from our high priest Jesus until He comes. Jesus' commission says,*" **All power is given to me in heaven and under. Go ye therefore, and teach all nations, baptizing them in the name of the Father, and of the Son, and of the Holy Ghost. teaching them to observe all things whatsoever I have commanded you, and lo I am with you always, even until the end of the world."** (Matthew 28:18,20)

The End

www.ingramcontent.com/pod-product-compliance
Lightning Source LLC
Chambersburg PA
CBHW051002050726
47592CB00007B/2679